Times Change

Going Shopping

Long Ago and Today

Lynnette R. Brent

Heinemann Library
Chicago, Illinois

© 2003 Heinemann Library
a division of Reed Elsevier Inc.
Chicago, Illinois

Customer Service 1-888-454-2279
Visit our website at
www.heinemannlibrary.com

Design by Herman Adler Design
Editorial Development by
Morrison BookWorks, LLC
Photo Research by Carol Parden,
Image Resources
Printed and bound in the United States by
Lake Book Manufacturing, Inc.

07 06 05 04 03
10 9 8 7 6 5 4 3 2 1

**Library of Congress Cataloging-in-
Publication Data**
Brent, Lynnette R., 1965-
Going Shopping: long ago and today /
Lynnette R. Brent.
   p. cm. -- (Times change)
Summary: An introduction to how shopping
has changed in the past one hundred years,
discussing how the places we go to shop
evolved from a general store to the Internet,
and how paying for items has changed.
Includes bibliographical references and index.
   ISBN 1-4034-4535-4 (Library Binding-hard-
cover) -- ISBN 1-4034-4541-9 (Paperback)
   1. Shopping--History--Juvenile literature.
[1. Shopping--History.] I. Title. II. Series.
   TX335.5.B74 2003
   380.1'45'000904--dc21
                                   2003011104

Acknowledgments
The author and publishers are grateful to
the following for permission to reproduce
copyright material: pp. 1(l), 5, 6(m-l), 12, 30(b-
m) Bettmann/Corbis, p. 1(r) Sears; pp. 6(b-r),
30(b-l) Sears Archives; p. 7 Patarick Olear/
PhotoEdit; p. 8 Schenectady Museum; Hall of
Electrical History Foundation/Corbis; p. 9
Stone/Getty Images; pp. 10(m-l), 14, 16, 20,
22(m), 24, 26(t), 28 Brown Brothers, p. 10(b-r)
Hulton Deutsch Collection/Corbis; p. 11 Alan
Schein Photography/Corbis; p. 13 Mark
Erickson/Getty Images; p. 15 Corbis; p. 16(b-
r) King Kullen Inc; p. 17 Ted Horowitz/Corbis;
p. 18 Robert Martin/Grapevine Antiques; pp.
19, 21 Corbis; pp. 22(b-r), 30(b-r) Minnesota
Historical Society; p. 23 Monika Graff/
The Image Works; p. 25 Bob Daemmrich/
The Image Works; p. 26(b-r) Smithsonian
Institution; p. 27 David Young-Wolff/PhotoEdit;
p. 29 Don Mason/Corbis

Cover photographs reproduced with
permission of (t) Brown Brothers, (b) Eric
Larreydieu/Getty Images

Every effort has been made to contact
copyright holders of any material reproduced
in this book. Any omissions will be rectified
in subsequent printings if notice is given to
the publisher.

Some words are shown in bold, **like this.**
You can find out what they mean by looking
in the glossary.

Contents

Long Ago

Imagine that it's long ago. You and your mother are waiting outside the new department store in your city. The store's grand opening is a very big event.

The doors to the store finally open. Your mother cannot believe all of the **products** she can find in one store. She used to shop in many different stores. Before the department store came to town, your parents also ordered things from a **catalog** and waited to get them. Shopping is going to be very different at a department store.

This is what you may have been thinking if you shopped 100 years ago. What kinds of things would you have bought if you lived long ago? How would you have paid for these things? Let's see what shopping was like in the United States long ago.

In 1893, this department store in Dayton, Ohio offered shoppers many choices of things to buy.

Different Ways to Shop

Long ago, people shopped in different ways. One popular way was to order from **catalogs**. Catalogs were helpful for people who lived far from cities. People who lived near cities usually shopped at small shops called general stores. People did not have many choices when they shopped.

Many people ordered long-lasting items, such as shoes, sewing machines, and furniture from catalogs.

Times Change

What Changed in 1925?

In 1925, Sears, Roebuck & Company opened its first department store in Chicago, Illinois. Before it opened, people ordered things from the catalog and waited for them to come in the mail.

At Sears, Roebuck & Company's first store people could touch and see products before buying them.

6

Today, there are many catalogs and plenty of stores to choose from. People often shop at big stores called department stores that offer a wide variety of **products.** Many people also buy things over the **Internet.** The Internet has made shopping easier because items can be purchased quickly and from all over the world.

Buying items on the Internet is similar to ordering from a catalog.

Where Did Goods Come From?

Long ago, goods were made in factories and sent to stores to sell. Goods are items that people want to buy. Many people had to work in the factories to make goods. Each person at the factory had one job to do. The goods were sometimes sent to other places by train.

Factories like this one needed many workers to do the same job over and over.

Today, goods are still made in factories. There are not as many workers in factories as there were long ago. Now, factories have many machines that make the goods. Machines can finish making goods much faster than factory workers can. Today, goods are sent to stores on trains, trucks, and airplanes.

Today, many factories need fewer workers because computers run the machines.

Advertising

Long ago, stores got people's attention with advertisements, or ads. Ads showed items that people could buy, and also brought attention to one type of store. Some stores mailed postcard advertisements to people. Other stores put ads in magazines and newspapers. Ads could also be found on big signs, called **billboards,** near roads.

Some stores had people wear sandwich boards to advertise goods.

Times **Change**

What Changed in 1941?

In 1941, television began showing its first advertisements before and after programs. Now, there are many advertisements on television and at the movies. Ads now reach many more people.

Television ads were used to sell things like dish washing soap.

Today, some billboards have bright, flashing lights to get people's attention.

Today, stores still use advertisements to get people's attention. Magazines, newspapers, and billboards continue to be popular places for advertisements. Stores also put advertisements on the radio and on television. These are the ways stores show people what they have to sell.

Attracting Shoppers

In 1912, these shoppers stopped for lunch at the department store's soda fountain.

Long ago, stores held special events so people would come and shop. Some stores had parades. Other stores opened tea rooms. A few even had lunch counters. When a store had a lunch counter, shoppers came and spent the whole day at the store. They could shop, eat lunch, and then shop some more!

Carnival rides attract shoppers to the mall so they will shop in the stores.

Today, stores have many different kinds of events to bring in shoppers. There are fashion and art shows for people to watch. Many stores have large sales that have holiday themes. Some stores even hold carnivals for people to enjoy.

Shopping for Clothes

Long ago, people did not shop for all of their clothes. Women made clothes for their families. They made the clothes with fabric they ordered from a **catalog.** Shoes were also ordered from a catalog or a shoemaker. Men bought suits and hats from a **tailor.** No matter where they came from, most of the clothes were made by people.

Long ago, women made clothes for themselves and their families.

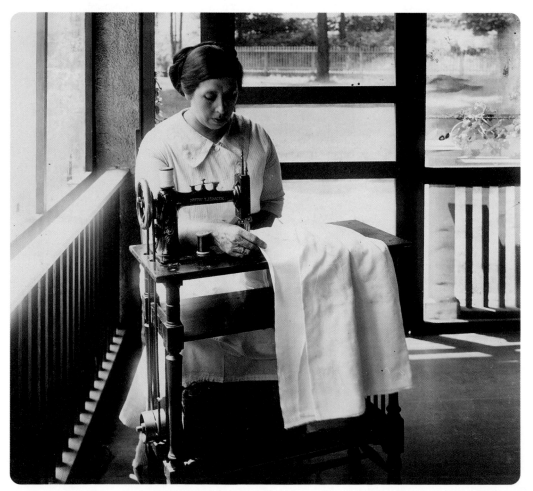

Today, people buy many of their clothes from big stores.

Today, not as many people make their own clothes. Instead, they buy clothes from stores. Large stores today have many kinds of clothes to choose from. Most clothes are made in factories by machines.

People can buy clothes from stores, catalogs, or over the **Internet.** These ways of shopping make buying clothes easier for many people.

Shopping for Food

Long ago, people bought only as many eggs as they needed for the day.

Long ago, people went to grocery stores to get food. The store's owner or a clerk would get the food and items the people needed. Grocery stores had very few choices for foods, fruits, and vegetables. People had to shop many times a week to get fresh foods, since there were no refrigerators to keep food cold.

Times Change

What Changed in 1930?

In 1930, the first grocery store opened where people could shop on their own. King Kullen grocery store opened in Queens, New York, on August 4, 1930.

This is the sign King Kullen uses today.

Today, many people buy large amounts of things and keep them at home until they are needed.

Today, grocery stores are much different. People can get groceries for themselves without help. They have many food choices. Grocery stores now have refrigerators and freezers to keep foods cold. Foods stay fresher longer so people do not need to go to the grocery store many times a week.

Shopping for Toys

Girls sometimes made dolls that looked like themselves.

Long ago, there were not many stores that sold toys. Many toys were made at home. Girls made dolls from old rags and boys built models of trucks and boats with whatever they could find. The few toys that were bought from stores included marbles and dishes for dolls.

Today, toys are sold everywhere! There are toy stores that sell everything from dolls to video games. Department stores and grocery stores even sell toys. Some people buy their toys over the **Internet** or from **catalogs.**

Today, most children do not make their own toys because they can buy them at toy stores.

Shopping for Gifts

People worked on homemade gifts all year long.

Long ago, gifts were homemade and were given on holidays. People took a great deal of time working on their gifts. Children would usually receive only one gift on their birthday. They would receive a few other gifts during other holidays. People did shop for a small amount of gifts from a **catalog** or from a nearby general store.

Today, some people still make gifts, but most gifts are bought from stores. Most stores today sell many different things for gift giving. People give gifts for special holidays and for birthdays. Some stores sell special gift items, like flowers, candy, and jewelry.

Today, people save time by buying gifts instead of making them.

Places to Shop

Long ago, people had to go to many stores to buy what they needed. Many stores sold only one kind of thing. When people went shopping, they stopped at a lot of different stores. A person who had a horse would get food from the feed store and horseshoes from the **blacksmith.** Shopping took a very long time.

People had to shop at many stores all over town to get the things they needed.

Times Change

What Changed in 1956?

In 1956, Southdale Shopping Center opened. Southdale Shopping Center was the first indoor mall to be built in the world.

Southdale Shopping Center opened in October 1956 in Edina, Minnesota.

Today, people can buy many of the things they need in one shopping trip. They can go to the mall! People can buy all kinds of things at a mall. Malls have different types of stores all in one building. They have clothing stores, food stores, jewelry stores, and even banks. People can save a lot of time by shopping at malls.

In a mall, people can shop at many stores in one place.

Taking a Break from Shopping

Long ago, after people did their shopping at their local general store, they would relax there. Many people would sit next to potbellied stoves and play checkers. Others would take time to talk about what was new in town. It was fun to relax at the general store after all the shopping was done.

People sat on crates and boxes so they could talk with friends in the general store.

Many malls offer places for people to sit and relax with friends.

Today, people can do many things in malls to relax when they are out shopping and need a break. People can sit and eat in food courts. There are movie theaters where people can see a movie. Some malls even have arcades where people can play video games. There is a lot to do at the mall when it's time to take a break.

Paying for Goods

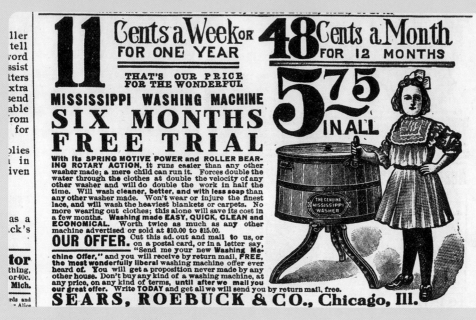

This ad from 1906 showed how people could buy things using credit.

Long ago, people paid for goods in many different ways. Most people paid with cash. Some people wrote checks that paid the store with money from their bank accounts. A few people bought things using credit. This meant they gave the store a little money each month until the **product** was totally paid for.

Times Change

What Changed in 1951?

In 1951, the first credit card to be accepted by stores across the country was issued. This card allowed people to buy things on credit from many stores.

The first Diners Club credit card was given to only 200 people.

Today, paying for goods is much like it was long ago. People still pay for things using cash and they still write checks from their bank accounts. Buying on credit is also still used. Today, the most popular way for people to pay for purchases is by using a credit card.

This store window shows some of the different credit cards people can use today.

Bringing Goods Home

Long ago, people did much of their shopping on foot. They walked from their homes to the store and got the things they needed. People bought food in small amounts because they had to carry it home. Some people bought things and had them delivered to their house. People bought ice this way a few times a week.

Ice was delivered on an ice wagon to people's homes.

Cars make it easier to bring things home from stores that are far away.

Today, cars make it easier to bring things home after shopping. People do not have to hand carry everything they buy, so they are able to buy more. Some people still have the things they buy delivered. Things that are ordered from **catalogs** or over the **Internet** can be delivered right to people's front doors.

You have seen how shopping has changed over time. Long ago, people did not have as many choices as they have today. Shopping was hard work! It took a long time to make and buy the things that a family needed. People today can shop in many different ways to buy the things they need. It's quicker, easier, and there are more things to choose from.

Times Change

1925	1930	1941	1951	1956
Sears, Roebuck & Company opens its first department store.	King Kullen grocery store opens.	Advertisements are first shown on television.	Diners Club issues the first nationally accepted credit card.	The first indoor mall opens in Edina, Minnesota.

Sears, Roebuck & Company

television advertisements

Southdale Shopping Center

Glossary

billboard flat surface on which advertisements are shown outside

blacksmith worker who shapes iron by heating it and then hammering it on an iron block

catalog book containing a list of items, and a picture of each with many details, that are in order according to a system

Internet system of information that connects computers together all over the world

product something that is made or produced

tailor person whose job is making or fixing clothes

More Books to Read

DiSalvo-Ryan, DyAnne. *Grandpa's Corner Store.* HarperCollins Children's Books. New York, NY, 2000.

McGovern, Ann. *If You Lived About 100 Years Ago.* Scholastic Inc. New York, NY, 1999.

Ask an older reader to help you read this book:

O'Hara, Megan. *General Store: A Village Store in 1902.* Blue Earth Books. Mankato, MN, 1998.

Index